Over

and

Up

Climb

Vines

Over
and
Up
Climb
Vines

Claudia McGill

Vines Climb Up and Over.

ISBN: 9781686357336

Cover Art:

Other Books by Claudia McGill

Poetry:

Look Winter in the Face
Spring Cleaning
Catch Up With Summer
Autumn Opens a Door
Twenty Minutes
Get to the Point
Enough For a Book
Compositions in Collage
Picking Up Pieces
Picture Making
Generous With the Details
Refuge
Repairs
Redirection
Rearrange
Clean Canvas
Vines Overpower Trellis and Run
Pink Chalk
Trailing Vines All Over the Place
Unpredictable Hue

Other Works:

The Journey to Survival: The Search for Moral Self-Awareness in the Works of Joseph Conrad (literary criticism)

Distractions Can Be Murder (mystery novel)

Minuscule (short stories/poetry)

Introduction

These tiny poems are written according to a formula –
each one must have three lines, or maybe four, but no
more.

That's it.

I write them in groups (there is a table at the back of
the book that lists them by date) and I do it this way:

To prepare for a session, I take notes – conversations,
TV dialogue, ads on the radio. I don't discriminate or
edit. I just write down phrases or sentences that I hear
and that interest me.

When I'm ready to write, I take out my notebook and I
make a list of appealing fragments. It's better to have
too many rather than too few choices.

Then I start to combine them. I use additional lines from
my notes, or I fill in with my own ideas.

When I've done enough, I stop.

It's best not to overthink the process. I don't go back
and work over the finished poems – it seems to take
the clarity and bite away from them. In pretty much
every case, second-guessing and rewriting only remove
the zing. I certainly don't want that. Instead, I move on
to a new set of poems when I want to say more.

I call these poems "Little Vines", from the word *vignette*. I thought *vignette* was too fancy; I liked the straightforwardness of these two words - Little Vines.

Now that I think about it, I guess the word *straightforward* is an odd one to think of in relation to these Vines, because it certainly doesn't describe anything about them but their name. No, Vines are twisty, as vines are. They go places, they find a way, and they get there fast, but they are not – straightforward.

Well, I'll leave it to you to read them and work your way through the turns and tangles. See what you think.

Claudia McGill
August 2019

Note about the Little Vines series:

Vines Climb Up and Over is the third volume of Little Vines, comprised of Vines 2007-3003.

Earlier books:

Vines Overpower Trellis and Run, 1-1004

Trailing Vines All Over the Place, 1005-2006.

Over
and
Up
Climb
Vines

2007.
they smelted metal night after night
you said it was a voodoo ritual
like you know anything about voodoo or smelting

2008.
the beach covered with sand
the ocean full of wet salty water
the beach towel wiggling its terrycloth loops

2009.
the ocean pushing up wet salty waves
it was an eerie green scene that I saw
after I drowned and lay on the bottom with sand
        in my hair.

2010.
I said I had sore muscles
He said run them through a copy machine
at the extra strength ink setting
See if that helps you next time.

2011.
a truck's horn
stunned my socks
they fell down around my ankles limp with terror

2012.
fingers curled around the yellow pencil
can we follow them
see what they write?

2013.
Of course I am certain she is holding a grudge
she has forty-five acres full of them in fact
she's won ribbons at the state fair for her
          grudge production

2014.
the doctor removed the stitches
said she'd be out to sea for a couple of days
just be patient she'll drift back in eventually

2015.
living in the family home
I always expect the worst
these people just don't give up

2016.
pretend you are not a chair
in the attic
promising nothing

2017.
everyone in polka dot pajamas
clustered around a restaurant buffet
the symbolism of the family photos really spoke to me

2018.
ok, I'm home now
so let's talk friction
so let's talk a hot-tempered stove frying up some
          free-range eggs

2019.
I think he went around back to check on the alligator
I made some coffee and waited
I knew before long I'd see his skinny bald head
on his shoulders or not and either way it would be ok
          with me

2020.
one of the living dead after nightfall
you're right things have changed recently
well, let's just say it's personal now

2021.
we are not used to such goings-on at the office
the poisoned spike we keep in the break room
has always worked up to now

2022.
it turns out he is one of the less than semi-good people
        living in apartment 310
she is the bellicose occupant of 314
Meanwhile here in 312 we cower

2023.
there are few safeguards available and though
I cannot predict lethal
false teeth in a gossipy mouth can produce quite
        an uproar

2024.
a free plane ticket in my pocket
and here I was
waiting at the bus stop

2025.
We don't have much sugar.
Traditional values in culinary activities of this sort
demand a sweeter outcome. Time to visit a neighbor.

2026.
eventually you get what is coming to you
I won't let you down
I'll make sure you get it

2027.
it's my turn to say hello
cake-baker full of surprises
and to slap you with a subpoena

2028.
a free plane ticket
the plane is on the runway
what are you waiting for?

2029.
dude, how was life
the booming voice asked
from somewhere out in the mist

2030.
it's illegal of course and highly predictive of jail time
the antidote is
no one ever uses a real name around here

2031.
once again I'm in big trouble here at home
so I guess we'd better start making some more soup
no need to salt it I will be crying into it soon

2032.
one great big ten-layer chocolate cake coming up
of course not at a moment's notice
I've got to translate the recipe from Norwegian
first I've got to learn Norwegian

2033.
the plumber sleeping in the bathtub
the carpet installer setting tack strips along
        the driveway
and the first words the postman said to me were:
don't worry no one has sent you a bill for the work yet.

2034.
so you are finally awake
I can tell by the power surge and exploding lights
let me call the electrician before you try to sit up

2035.
either there is a lot or else there is none
the limitations of the pattern
are not fixed and nor are they in good repair

2036.
come out zombies and conquer your new world
late last night after so much planning the papers signed
the taxes paid. It's all yours.

2037.
three months in the same room
talking business with that woman non-stop
it all seems to go back to one enchanting memory.

2038.
the air glittered
made a tremendously good impression
on our lungs and circulatory systems

2039.
en garde you arthritic turtle
step up here and show me what you've got
though I have time to wait for only so long

2040.
abducted by two very busy kidnappers
sorry, we're overbooked they said
paid me to go home and keep my mouth shut

2041.
there is no key
in the ignition
of the alien heat ray. I'll have to hot-wire it.

2042.
You and the fans and the reporters
A white-gloved hand waving from the limousine
A lightning strike. A sudden silence.

2043.
the aliens came here as medical tourists
Five million US dollars later
every one of them went home looking like Dolly Parton

2044.
Our store is called The Ark: we sell
two tutus striped in red sequins
twin bad afternoons
flatworms, yes, we do have a pair

2045.
no more gruel for me, please
the air pressure in this neighborhood
turns it chunky and then it wiggles.

2046.
I'm as terrified as you are by the results
a thorough forensic analysis of modern suburbia
AKA spelunking through the rusted-out minivan

2047.
add two and two
there's nobody better at this game than your brother
first grade really did do its job

2048.
gray and cream floor tiles
wrapped around a pallid cubicle worker
installed in a twenty-story concrete office ziggurat

2049.
the doctor retired three months ago
one hundred years old and counting
His mother drove him to the farewell party

2050.
my boyfriend cooked the meatloaf perfectly
his infrared eyes
came through for us once again

2051.
fake grins all around
residual effect
of being fooled big-time and in public

2052.
why this sheep is still here
I do not know
I think her car has broken down

2053.
three poisonous frogs
in the mud
grinning and snapping at your toes

2054.
there is only one solitude
it will not be enough
for all of you who want it

2055.
I didn't exactly make a decision yet
where to aim the bolt of lightning
It's such a fine balance between "need" and "deserve"

2056.
all of us are innocent enough
walking on broken glass
one minute from being struck by a meteor

2057.
employed by a firm here in town
expensive coat she's wearing
she's going to make one angry ghost

2058.
I wasted a bucket of spackle on the kitchen ceiling
after the fellow from the UFO
fell through the roof

2059.
all the fancy neon famous
all the schemers who became class president
all the fugitives who blew the roadblock

2060.
she came back as a memory
illusion wrapped in a pink pearl necklace
opera-length.

2061.
Once I spent two weeks
stuck to the side of a satellite north of the Moon
I just could not get my earrings to de-magnetize

2062.
So many vampires
lying on the beach
in the pitch dark

2063.
a man at the door
an intruder
once he stepped across the threshold

2064.
you want rules I'll give you rules
the barbed wire fence
tear-your-skin-to-shreds kind of certainties

2065.
the taxi driver in a deep sleep
the rice that has not yet boiled over
the unopened flowers in the bridal bouquet

2066.
I guess that's a yes
most of it fell to the floor
but what about all of it that did not?

2067.
How close we came to
not one not two but twenty-two
one drunken weekend forty years ago

2968.
the shop smelled cold and green
the flowers stood stiff and icy
from what unfriendly garden could they have come?

2069.
All I did was walk in the door
into yet another awkward situation
at mile marker seventeen

2070.
you say good-bye on the eve of the estate sale
to kitschy trinkets that you know are thinking
trust me I'm not going to disappear this easily

2071.
up all night with the baby
it was just business as usual
sometimes I think nothing but spirit possession can
        explain it

2072.
on the street corner
in the fog
the work of a skilled florist
upside down in a trash can

2073.
it was only a few hours
everything is so different now
goodness what a day you've had

2074.
green and frozen stiff
in the ice
a dropped mitten

2075.
I keep having these dreams where you know they're
        going to chase you
up to the brink of the edge of the rim of the sheer
        vertical drop
into the laundry tub full of suds

2076.
oh dear the trap door won't hold any longer
my mother shouted
I'll try to call you with better news next time

2077.
Run I shouted but you
were already possessed and
proud of it

2078.
radishes in the salad, no
cash in the laundry room, no
two newly-dead people in the living room, no
I know nothing of any of it.

2079.
some of us were hiding
a long way from home
on stage in full makeup

2080.
the elephant of impermeability crossed
the river of complaints
in a jiffy

2081.
the two of us
alive
proved the value of the risk

2082.
Swim to the shore I shouted
I didn't
and look where that got me

2083.
A junkyard and
seven hundred
motorcycle fragments

2084.
getting ready to hibernate
planning and patience, yes, but
really, it's a nice change of pace

2085.
don't underestimate me
daily life disaster that I am
I'm the one who's been calling your name

2086.
So cold, the young man said
So invigorating
The best day of my life.

2087.
all quiet in here
the two brains in one head
and both of them asleep at the same time

2088.
we go way back
but it isn't the same thing
as being old friends

2089.
a deadbeat office drone
a cheap radio
both get through the day with a lot of effort though
        with little focus

2090.
Remember that I have the same reasons as you have
I'm doing this for you
So are you

2091.
so that's a funny story actually
but not one that I should tell
outside my own head

2092.
wait a little longer
a cat's birthday
doesn't come around every day

2093.
you say the non-moving limo needs a new transmission
so please just answer the question
the kid on the bike – is he my new chauffeur?

2094.
Memory loss
are you for real
please notify me in writing

2095.
we'll figure it out
the vehicles of memory are parked in the same garage
though they all seem to be leaking oil

2096.
It's taking a lot of effort
in order to meet all my obligations
That is why I push them further back in the desk drawer

2097.
you don't actually think
it was ever going to balance
here, right on my long pointed nose?

2098.
idiots can be found anywhere
go for the cheapest one
we're not really that worried about the quality

2099.
any jackpot
any size
never goes out of style

2100.
the astronaut was lonely for any news of Earth
give my regards to the next human you meet
she said to the moon

2101.
no I'm just worried you are not in the parking lot
I am thinking you might be lost or stolen alas
little red car I love so well

2102.
thanks for the cash, said the grifter
I took it off your hands
so you'd be less encumbered by the material world

2103.
I cash in the lottery ticket
an ordinary lady now glittering in the fluorescent lights
of the convenience store

2104.
I'm wearing sunglasses
against my will
in a complicated algorithm I don't fully understand
          even now

2105.
I will pay cash for two of your teeth
right
now.

2106.
the field of corn surrounding my blue house
it's making me a little tense
being observed all the time

2107.
the itinerary full of very detailed instructions
yet impossible to make a connection to the map
so was I here yesterday or not?

2108.
so the social worker was operating undercover
it could be any one of us in his shoes
yet it was not

2109.
I maintain a look of concern on my face
but
I am an entirely different person now

2110.
say a prayer lay a wreath
my old man
covered in dirt
his toes inside his best shoes pointing at the sky

2111.
stop spending money focus your attention
and if you need to splurge
take a bath and use up all the hot water

2112.
Cook anything you like
over a campfire on the beach
I tell you it will taste mouthwatering times ten

2113.
a replenishment
of my favorite ear-twitch powder -
when is enough ever enough?

2114.
education is just so expensive
I was going to be a blue star sparkling in the sky
instead I am a silver foil Christmas tree standing
        in the mall

2115.
everyday life
pummeled her intelligence
wrecked her brain

2116.
I am a messenger
bearing bad news
thank goodness I know CPR

2117.
the facts are lining up
ready to march
and still the one eye sees and the other one does not

2118.
I separated it into batches but
if that ends it
no one will be more surprised than I am

2119.
Applauding
the very well-kept teeth
the dentist waived his fee this visit

2120.
fallen silent
just when I thought
you could be counted on

2121.
the sunshine
paying some attention
to the cacti
so late in the afternoon

2122.
Finding a friendly face
in the silence of this street
such a remote possibility

2123.
dropped
the photograph with a secret
on the floor

2124.
to put it more succinctly
in contrast to limp spinach
this guy sitting next to me is eye candy

2125.
the windows open and all I wanted
was to have a sight of
summer

2126.
hold that thought
it's not real it's just not real
just stick to that story and you'll be ok

2127.
now that we know you better
a single man living in Apartment 4B
the rules are suspended

2128.
Displacement along the fault line:
sometimes you've got to make changes.
The question is when it is too much?

2129.
we rented space
in a storage warehouse
now we need to fill it up with thoughts

2130.
in a locked container
good evening and I'm beginning to wonder
no escape this time?

2131.
and where else would I be but
drinking beer at the dining room table
in a snowstorm

2132.
yeah but you don't like that music
yeah but it never mattered to me until now
yeah because now I don't like it either

2133.
I got my hair cut
I couldn't live like that
in that miserable dank tower

2134.
I'm sorry and good luck there
the symptoms are progressing
next time you see me
you'll find me in the crowd at the reading of your will

2135.
pink and red
so where did you appear from
bouquet of zinnias?

2136.
in the middle
somehow we manage
but it's all kind of a blur

2137.
cut out the boo hoo
you're not such a loser as all that
yet

2138.
oh you sneaked out the real you
you left this other you behind
will this you be here long enough
for us to get to know any of you?

2139.
don't look at it you said.
that's not the answer I wanted.
ok I admit so maybe I should not have looked.

2140.
speaking of the neighbors
I've always known I would want to say good-bye
        to them
in a memorable way

2141.
oh how clear
my pale blue eyes
how deep their surveillance of you

2142.
in this room full of people
I'm counting on you
a loner with a bouffant hairdo and bad breath?

2143.
full of raisins and nuts
the cake said
why don't you come in for a closer look?

2144.
I'm not going to hide anymore
Look in this direction
You will see me behind the window peering out

2145.
I have a concussion
I need to call a tow truck
I'll see you in the morning
OK?

2146.
one look in this direction
a mere twelve seconds
results: we fell in love we got married we had
        three kids

2147.
the engine
persuades the rest of the car
to move

2148.
I washed my hair five times on the tenth of January
I don't want to talk about any other day in my life
Nothing else has ever lived up to that experience

2149.
I feel a sense of relief at the asteroid strike
it's not a permanent solution
but it gets me out of babysitting

2150.
in the original score
you meet me at the loading dock
we dance and then we unload a truck

2151.
more than a bit of fabric and wire
the umbrella was a friend
we were together for fifteen years

2152.
fair warning
I am
sensational inside and out

2153.
skating rink turned pink rink let's think
pink tissue paper pink smoke pink drinks
what a bachelorette party it was

2154.
The headache
takes a look around
chooses the lady with red hair and glasses

2155.
We'll both get what we want
but this time
the smile won't be enough to do it

2156.
That was number seventeen
and how is that possible
when fifteen is all there are in the world?

2157.
and suddenly the stranger
is a friend
a souvenir of that long-ago vacation

2158.
the nurse just making sure
you still looked nervous
as a patient awaiting a double root canal should be

2159.
the glue
an enemy
to the unfast and loosened

2160.
so it's all wrong
this silence
interrupted by the ringing in my ears

2161.
no no make it stop
how could you do that to me
sing those words to that tune and today of all days?

2162.
Monday Wednesday Friday
Today is Thursday
it's perplexing how this week has suddenly fallen
      into pieces

2163.
after that time last winter
when a thousand and one
icicles hung on the eaves

2164.
come out
in disbelief
stay and marvel

2165.
why don't you come in for a closer look
you clever little creature
This stuff is really potent. You will love it.

2166.
as for veering off into serious double vision -
it's not worrying over nothing, is it,
to see two giant lizards reaching for your
        steering wheel?

2167.
oh that poor fellow
went out through the cat flap
anything to avoid babysitting for those kids tonight

2168.
the choice
the impulse
to leave home
before I was torn to shreds

2169.
a peace offering, my foot
you are a fraud full of muscle spasms
and a broken metatarsal is more like it

2170.
I hear you breathing
holding your breath
breathing again

2171.
It was a long time ago
I didn't have the best reputation
What a vile stench it was, in fact

2172.
no second thoughts
we're still on for tonight
the impulse still strong and the heart still beating

2173.
you know perfectly well
a green person with green eyes
shouldn't be swimming in the fountain at the park
it's just too cold for it at this time of year

2174.
interesting first day at work
it turned out to be
take the money and drive away fast with a great
        group of guys

2175.
I was a loner but calling it quits
I started playing trombone in a band at the BBQ joint
drink up and dance I say drink up and dance

2176.
The loyalty that is colored in deep blue shades
I don't want to be blamed
for the fading that occurs over time

2177.
We have unfinished business?
I'm just not so sure.
What makes you so sure?

2178.
the kind of situation this is
easy to find out
hard to understand

2179.
in the dark
I was quite certain
this street was not entirely free of ectoplasmic
        skid marks

2180.
is this a test
where you can finally learn why
being discontented is so appealing?

2181.
because I specialize in contemporary work
the medieval monk scam was a stretch for me
short order cook dishing up contraband chili -
    no problem

2182.
my apologies for interfering
but that semi-dead body in the front hall
what are you going to do about it?

2183.
as I examined every inch
the windows and the ceiling and the kitchen drawers
darling you have no idea
how much I used to trust you

2184.
not doing anything illegal
but I am living with a secret
a lonely echoing voice that only I can hear

2185.
offering the kind of help that is
a little too showy
definition of a co-worker who wants my job

2186.
a person we never expected to see again
the guy who had knocked out his front teeth on my
        mother's scones
decontaminated and green but not pressing charges

2187.
societal upheaval
some of it I like
most of it I'm indifferent

2188.
A hypnotic marimba run
up and down the scales
It was one night a long time ago
I will never forget it. Never.

2189.
definition of imposter:
a whole other person
that you aren't

2190.
I am self-awareness
clothed in a black linen sheath dress
I am that ancient amphibian seeking out prey

2191.
twin souls
face to face
we are like night and more night

2192.
what do you remember about way back when
other than
it was all a long time ago?

2193.
we've all switched identities so many times
and now you know if anything happens to me
you will not be sure of it

2194.
taxidermy is not often so useful
though it was a good starting point for us
married thirty-two years in June, we are

2195.
the pale pink tomato
in a state of shock
failing the BLT job interview

2196.
shivering suitcases and storage bins with pneumonia:
a little reminder
we need to insulate the attic

2197.
what can I tell you
about our new backstabbing group
other than our motto: "let's put it all behind you".

2198.
Mirthful at the macabre joke
Guffawing as we inhale the noxious smell
coming from our brother's birthday cake

2199.
oh yeah we're sisters all right
encrypted and encoded
how well we know each other

2200.
we left home and we came here
my twin sister and me
two comets side by side in the sky

2201.
abrupt and so cold
you have perfected that expression
how well you know me and what will persuade me

2202.
watch closely the three moons in the sky
somehow two of them got involved and then
one day there was a third

2203.
These days
I'm living my dreams
with some parts blacked out

2204.
please come home
natural vs. synthetic
no longer matters to me

2205.
I've run out of time
burned out my electrical circuits.
One too many of the wrong people have come into
	my life.

2206.
worst of all
I'm sure I know what you mean
when you say the refrigerator seems to have serious
    breathing issues

2207.
not to discipline the yarn but to coax it
not to tell the story but to ask it
This is my advice to you.

2208.
gossipy old men
they all say the same thing
once they finally find themselves in the afterlife

2209.
Don't play stupid
Faking tears in a victory speech
only makes your mascara run

2210.
stop messing with my head
my hair looks fine
touch it again and I'll submit a claim for damages

2211.
the very lonely pie
due to its taste
the only thing left in the derelict spaceship

2212.
Bio-hazardous BBQ restaurant
the diners' green glowing teeth
smiling next to their half-eaten sandwiches

2213.
give me five minutes just five minutes
with that four-layer meatloaf
I'm not afraid to test my limits

2214.
fragile and complicated
you have a bright future
you could be dangerous to me.

2215.
the mathematics of my thinking are running in circuits
my concentration exists in an eternal looping and
buzzing
may the tiny nails hold firm.

2216.
I'm in a hurry you said
and just like that
we were strangers again.

2217.
It's this one
really too small
that I like the best

2218.
that's the first lesson
in the middle of the night
when you hear a noise downstairs
don't get up

2219.
Never mentioned it.
Never talked about it.
It never occurred. It never occurred.

2220.
what now she screeched
as the room cracked open
from floor to ceiling

2221.
writing found two thousand years from now
tax records and love notes and grocery lists
ancient words drawn in indelible ink

2222.
who cares where the baby is
and what difference does it make to you anyway
if she stays out all night again?

2223.
a tailwind
from a few fat electrons
running from a light bulb bent on capturing them

2224.
just business as usual
power up the heat ray blow away the aliens
do it again on Tuesday. On Wednesday. On Thursday.

2225.
Go into a library?
I think I'm pretty clever
but I'm so afraid to test the limits

2226.
Don't pay any attention
to that smooth-voiced guy full of good cheer
blaming all the trouble on me

2227.
how much do you know about
the pain of a social castaway who's just been told:
There's only room for one of us in this town?

2228.
those two are crazy in love
I was so pleased with myself
there are all kinds of spells, aren't there

2229.
I resolve to hold my breath
ask those odoriferous questions
recover my sanity at the cost of my olfactory nerves

2230.
he is a refrigerator in need of a change:
long peaceful nights
the urge to break down recurring each morning
        at breakfast

2231.
persistence
said the little brown snail
laying down a trail of silver

2232.
Quick where can I get that enzyme
Subtle, obnoxious, and so radioactive
The one that drives the men wild?

2233.
Son, when I tell you
keep your eye on the ball
it doesn't mean the other two can just sit and rest

2234.
You bet those are teeth marks
that's exactly why I need a bus ticket
pronto

2235.
my calculations were not worth a pad of graph paper
you knew about it yes you did
yet you climbed into the rocket and turned the key

2236.
despite everything I ever told you
I'm so glad to be back
at my stainless-steel dissecting table

2237.
isolation is the beginning
a period of reasonable safety is next
Then a power surge and your perm is done

2238.
knowing who your friends are
it might be a good time
to leave town

2239.
the aspirin tablet you are just about to step on
so what the kitchen floor did it no harm.
clean off the dust bunnies and give it to me.

2240.
stand up
get your balance
drop that alibi and try this one instead

2241.
a plus-size multi-layer party going on
at my neighbor's house
disguised as a garage sale

2242.
Maybe I haven't been as attentive as I should be
for a real long time
Or maybe I have. I forget.

2243.
let's get one thing straight
I'll pick you up at the bus depot
but I'm not including your lizard boyfriend in the offer

2244.
now we've got a bigger problem than we thought
the electrons did it again and disappeared
why can't you ever remember to close the door?

2245.
You remember what I told you
I told you to install a new guard for the lawnmower.
I guess your three-toed feet tell the rest of that story.

2246.
before I agree
let's have a look at those long thin fingers
that are going to have to draw those sweet
      little sketches

2247.
explaining the exact nature of
what we do in that dance class
it is just impossible

2248.
I have told you and told you
the silverware
is charging by the hour now. Eat faster.

2249.
The red cereal bowl
The huge mouth
gnawing its rim with blunt-edged teeth

2250.
no wallet no keys no cellphone
a rotted zucchini clutched in his hands
that's the story I heard, anyway

2251.
provoke an argument
waver your voice edge close to tears
passive aggression really can work in so many
        circumstances

2252.
on the one hand
I had a shipment of patience sent to me
on the other hand
I declined to use it

2253.
venture into this little ray of sunlight
within six minutes
you will be a grilled cheese sandwich

2254.
set herself adrift in the raucous party
wearing a dress of some shiny slippery fabric
she slithered through some interesting conversations

2255.
another two weeks of rain
we all go mad and mildewed
an unstoppable combination and I just can't wait

2256.
another ten years
nobody here
will be any smarter

2257.
in the intense cold
I feel the presence
of a very lonely man

2258.
she was asleep in the armchair
her frilled collar
filled with cookie crumbs

2259.
embroidery stitches
done at a terrifying pace
fibrous and aggressive

2260.
daytime's forced neutral
passing into your sleep
you no longer dream in color

2261.
sincerity this afternoon and lies tonight
pinpoint the moment when the changeover occurred
per person per day

2262.
the knitting needles offered
no assurances and warranties
against ugly or ill-fitting garments

2263.
soon we'll be going home
I could not get used to the idea
I wonder if the rosebushes are still there?

2264.
behind the glass panes
the patient lay in a splenic trance
null and void

2265.
Pssst, you, yes, you
you old fussbudget
let me flambé your inhibitions

2266.
how impossible
the mythology
but how infinitely comforting

2267.
spaghetti crazy
noon and still no lunch
the children took their vengeance

2268.
the doctor calling me the wrong name
as he sharpened the needle
I know I signed a contract but still

2269.
Flattery is certainly welcome
I'm not exempt from the effects of flattery
Call me anytime. I'd be flattered.

2270.
I warn you
a tree that gives off a vibe like this one
it forces you to accept your inferiority. Stand clear.

2271.
stood on a chair to look
not exactly sure
where I had stored the last syllable of that word

2272.
what a brainwave
what a beautiful idea
how did you let it get away?

2273.
four days four years ago we were so in love
I've never forgotten
that second-rate motel with the view of the
       fish hatchery

2274.
it all started when we stopped for lunch
I was in a lot of pain because you did not love me
I swallowed a lot more than my pride that day
vomited it up on the side of the road

2275.
the car is leaking oil
farting out fumes in the garage
and you say this car got you a speeding ticket?

2276.
now what
said the parakeet
with a hoarse cough

2277.
the nurse came into the room
a unique and mesmerizing woman
certainly more than my medical insurance
        bargained for

2278.
a runaway thunderstorm
lightning struck the ancient tree
pink and yellow flames were its last words

2279.
the television
in the darkened room
irritable and hallucinating

2280.
the stories are starting to blur together
absorbed one into the other
the reminiscences merge into the fairy tale I wished
        I'd lived

2281.
one day very soon
on our pesticide-free front lawn
they will get married
those two herbivores

2282.
if you'd like to make plans
Right now I am headed for grievous trouble
I'll get there sometime tomorrow mid-morning

2283.
This Valentine's Day reflect upon your feelings
for the man standing before you
a bouquet of cold-bitten grocery store roses in hand

2284.
a very through cynic
I had hoped I could change him
Peel that sour lemon
sprinkle him with sugar

2285.
a stolen watch
an unsealed envelope
you decide to turn a blind eye one more time

2286.
it's just work stuff and so boring
tough to explain and the kind of thing
that makes you lose your appetite

2287.
figuratively I got carried away
literally I'm up on libel and slander charges
moral of the story: pay attention to those pesky words

2288.
the last four days
the rate of change
I never had a beard before. What next?

2289.
it is dimly possible
in a thousand years
but no way this Valentine's Day

2290.
I see a practical woman
no intention of bringing trouble
until someone offered her a reward for it

2291.
the monsters have come back this year
now we're up to thirty
I guess we'll have to expand the table in the
     living room

2292.
a source of pride to the kitchen
the presence of a masterful cook
with a very active sense of spicy and piquant

2293.
my gardening chores squeezing me and distressing
     the garden
I'd rather be a tiny lizard sunning itself
let the garden decide its own style

2294.
my suggestion
mix up the paperwork
there is something about a good flummox
it takes the pressure off

2295.
I don't give up
I just slow it down
until I can catch hold of it

2296.
that one stubborn chili pepper
if only someone had put a tracker on it
before it got loose and obliterated your stomach

2297.
no I won't do it
unless you tell me
you'd rather do it

2298.
I signed the papers
handed over the key to the treasure box
Sorry but my non-disclosure agreement prohibits
        saying more

2299.
I let the robot translate.
Once I understood I said:
I'd be delighted but not until after lunch.

2300.
The death threat and
I think I've got good news for you
It's nothing personal. Just business.

2301.
a memorial service
for her artificial identity
the virtual life can be so cruel

2302.
You are way out-of-bounds
you not-so-model citizen of the Pliocene
This is my cave. Now scram.

2303.
wait I hear the bus backfiring right now
leaking oil at the corner stop
quick pack up that suitcase and get out there

2304.
Our family color is pink
Our family style is aiding and abetting
No focus group needed. We know what we like.

2305.
every night
in negotiations with our dreams
we ask and answer questions

2306.
Listen up
the dentist said
It's a simple day-long procedure

2307.
so who cares
it's just one page missing
a silent space in the midst of cacophony

2308.
that cute little baby smiling at you
oh she's smart all right
and a determined double crosser

2309.
of course I interrupted the doctor
she was doing it all wrong
it's the can opener first then the chainsaw

2310.
the rainbow a fugitive
laughing in your face
while you look for gold footprints

2311.
splish-splash
fresh and clean
the baby one minute after her bath

2312.
how about you drop in sometime
you beautiful blue fluid going by the name of ink
settle yourself in a comfortable fountain pen
we will sing a duet on paper

2313.
not everyone is selfish
skittish
or a survivor

2314.
Oh I know someone
very successful at altering opinions
embracing this new way of doing things

2315.
I'm trying to pull it all together
test me one more time
darn whatever the answer is
it just ran out the back door of my mind

2316.
the most delicate dental operation
surrender is everything says the dentist
you will feel better in a twitch of your eyelid

2317.
flu shot
opponents of regime change
sign up for battle

2318.
I disappeared on us.
I take it we're no longer friends.
I get that.

2319.
too-full trash cans
make no mistake about it
I deal with it but I sure as hell don't like it

2320.
on duty at the beanstalk dental clinic
it was just my luck
the ogre's tooth was abscessed

2321.
walk in the snow
I was so squeamish
about the yellow parts

2322.
you need to understand
I'm using my name
in a more recent configuration
than that under which you first met me

2323.
once you transfer the money to my bank account
I'm not so sure anymore
you'll stay a healthy old man

2324.
like a cloud
bleached white
and fraying

2325.
knees bent arms askew
you are not a natural ballerina
even after a few glasses of champagne

2326.
How our relationship is going:
we are taking things slowly
with a pinch of pepper

2327.
socialites do not
go home on the bus
even after a few glasses of champagne

2328.
I was in so deep too deep
shafts of light cutting through the green water
dimming as I sank

2329.
I asked for it
I've taken a special interest in it
I don't understand it

2330.
The pot of pink geraniums
isolated in the middle of the table
Am I interrupting you?

2331.
every two seconds in the garage
the hydraulic lift farts
you can do nothing but laugh

2332.
it's impossible
to stop the birds in that north-flying flock
I am glad.

2333.
we made such a long trip just to end up here
a fat pug dog lying on the rug
loud music coming from next door

2334.
that dear old friend
she never forgave me
once she understood what I was capable of

2335.
A greenhouse full of two-inch seedlings.
A lanky fellow wearing sunglasses.
I do not underestimate him.

2336.
go with me or stay behind
little spiders
it's not my place to tell you
but I hope -

2337.
are you going to tell me
we have never met before
I say and
the sisters close their eyes

2338.
when I was a child
come here I'm serious
meant *get ready for a switching on my bare legs*

2339.
all my secrets
taking sides
against me

2340.
it's not my fault a red shirt
infiltrated the tighty whities
leaving a laundry room full of shrinky pinkies

2341.
you have become so aggressive
half-open window
since you snapped your last sash cord

2342.
poor sad fellow wearing sunglasses
not a single hair on his head
ten million of them in his ears

2343.
you want a chance to make it right
you add it to the list
we'll see if it makes the cut

2344.
the polka dots had no other choice
rising up against argyle-patterned clothing
sign and countersign in competition for rack space

2345.
fraud in a red dress
crunching candy with her back teeth
getting impatient

2346.
no one knows
the smell of paste wax
like the floor in the second-grade classroom

2347.
A tightwad trillionaire
socialite satellites in orbit
establishing an alibi

2348.
scarcely a cup of motor oil
and already
I can wiggle my toes

2349.
the congenitally-headless store mannequin
betrayed and exploited
last seen sticking feet-up out of a dumpster

2350.
pterodactyl
in the corner office
guarding a nest egg or two

2351.
one minute friendly and next minute
a beautiful raptor
swallowing you whole

2352.
he is moving slowly on foot
circling
my sense of humor

2353.
a nasty headache and warts on your ears
because you took a little drink of that juice
life in a malevolent fairy tale

2354.
the strains of laundry day
the shenanigans the iron gets up to
the sneers of stains that refuse to vacate dress shirts
the eternal smell of baked starch in your hair

2355.
a lime green bowling ball just about to make a strike
rows and rows of white bowling shoes
snapping their shoelaces in a wave pattern. Hooray!

2356.
history and science crib notes
a slush fund
for your brain

2357.
a couple of golfers
their second shots on the eighth hole
blurred by a sudden storm of look-alike hail

2358.
all your brothers will drink martinis
create scenes at cocktail lounges
call you late at night for a ride home
so the ancient texts predict

2359.
exams coming up
panic flew in the window
settled in a crib and started to make notes

2360.
If you need proof
the creatures have returned to their roosts
Just look the employee locker room is empty

2361.
wait here
I'm no friend of hers
but I hate to hear a person cry like an old shoe who
      has lost its mate

2362.
a little overexcited
the antenna pulled in a signal
from her metal hair curlers

2363.
a crowd of gawkers calling out insults
perched on the roof of the golf clubhouse
never underestimate the birds and what they know

2364.
The tranquilizer dart hit me square in the leg.
Splintered my leg.
My Danish Modern leg. I am a table. Still, ouch.

2365.
in just a few short minutes
the spinning brushes of the luster-crazy floor buffer
atomized the linoleum

2366.
well-lit basement
the fading sound of skittering feet
oh they'll be back just turn off the light and wait

2367.
About this snowstorm
what an ineffective attempt at disruption it was
I think they let the second string have a try at it

2368.
The surprise hailstorm
some charming news
for the local windshield-replacement franchise

2369.
We've got four legs and we are carnivorous
Take my advice
Bow down to us

2370.
the meeting this morning
the big game
assembling in the conference room
sitting targets

2371.
what a skinflint you are
leaving no footprints leading away from here
you took them with you to use again

2372.
three o'clock when school ended
the beginning of a pleasant sense of holiday
that would last until eight AM the next day

2373.
there are calendars everywhere
one day
they just stopped working

2374.
I think I said
given a choice
I would rather not bite down hard just now

2375.
here is some humiliating news
we're breaking up on Valentine's Day
I've already reserved the time slot

2376.
a little silence
then
the sound of insect feet on the concrete

2377.
a giant twisting worm
hanging from the crane
poised over the construction site

2378.
none of the windows open in this office
no one
will hear you scream

2379.
You know when I was a kid
I was always wondering
Am I supposed to understand any of that?

2380.
swimsuit and goggles
that was always an option
but still the answer is no

2381.
so what do we do now
heading south on route sixteen
you with your pale cold blue eyes in the back of
        your head

2382.
broke a whole crate of clay pots
smashed his fingers in the door
A good day's work. Maybe he should rest a while.

2383.
Prehistoric in appearance and
programmed and hypnotized and mesmerized
one shout from me and all of them will come a' runnin'

2384.
oh what a cute baby you are
the best boss any of us has ever had
Kiss kiss.

2385.
a cruel woman
a quirky caper
now we stand behind the yellow line of police tape

2386.
a high-strung group of live-wires
full of electricity and magnetism
living in harmony
residents of the basement circuit box

2387.
you with the big mouth
now you need to go in there and bite
because that is one handsome piece of pecan pie

2388.
I mention the fourteenth
there could be any number of them of course
but I'm talking about the fourteenth

2389.
in the main dining room
a cloud of pink and yellow gas
the building is infested with blowhards all right

2390.
What were things like back then
before I was your stepsister
and I smashed your fingers in the door?

2391.
I spend all my time studying
I won't allow even a smidge of interference
the smoking electrical wires in my brain notwithstanding

2392.
take the stairs to the twelfth floor
in eleven seconds?
Someone's going to the afterlife tonight all right

2393.
take the stars to the twelfth planet
there's not much time
and it's the last one left

2394.
We made this deal a long time ago.
Clean things up resolve the balance
when I said.
Now I say.

2395.
the building shakes
the architect and her blueprints wince
the minor detail rears its ugly head

2396.
it's not under control
this mirage of chemistry
we have decided to call it love at first sight

2397.
crawling through the ventilation system
toward a promising career?
I don't know why I fell for this one.

2398.
I'm guessing this cold shoulder is about me yelling
hey you what's your name there again
at you my wife of forty-five years

2399.
even the most sensible attire
it's still a risk
have you noticed that your sweater is unraveling?

2400.
in lazy slow trickles
the good old days
bled out

2401.
Find out what it means
end her future
ok?

2402.
three waiters
my first husband
the sound of breaking glass

2403.
a lovely interchange between the two
desperate and delicate
the worm on the hook
the fish in the creek

2404.
I'm very fond of him
him strutting around the barnyard
wearing a high-style headgear
It's a cockle-doodle-doo do.

2405.
close enough old friend
don't take that last step
a kick in the shin can't be taken back

2406.
on your toes, folks
sometimes a bad day
circles back and bites again

2407.
Let me help you understand
this sink full of soap suds
how you fit in with its career ambitions

2408.
don't expect me to forgive you
it's the one thing
my insurance policy won't pay for

2409.
I think I had hopes
you were captivated by my apology
but my goodness you laughed me out of the room

2410.
I wish you'd never told me
what made you change your mind
move on to another line of work

2411.
I brought my brother along
this is a man you don't want to know
the last good news he heard was five years ago

2412.
I never met her before today
she was nothing to do with me
bet you five bucks we'll be married this time next year

2413.
take the risk
listen to me
forgive me

2414.
you are a person with no heart
you had a heart attack
something that today's science cannot explain

2415.
I'm not someone who enjoys explaining
in the conversational way
so just familiarize yourself with this great big hug

2416.
never see you hear you smell you again
I take a scalpel
I cut our friendship in two

2417.
I crossed a line
measured it out at seven and a quarter
I made just one copy
mailed it to you. Don't cry now.

2418.
this here's my older brother
I'm looking straight at him
congratulations to me I'm bigger than he is now

2419.
how happy they are together
all they do is shreds of strings
and falling through the loops

2420.
filling out the paperwork
two straight weeks of lying
no end in sight

2421.
went outside for some fresh air
I heard the tree ask the sky:
when will you bring my sunshine?

2422.
cinnamon buns
because I need a favor
some new towels
because she'll need to wash her sticky hands

2423.
her sharp mind and big muscles
she kicked me in the heart and I fell
in love

2424.
paying bills
it was merely a gesture
I knew I'd be gone before the checks bounced

2425.
the routine
that keeps the order
that keeps the sun floating in the sky

2426.
fixated and complicated
sitting beside the pool
I've been lonely for so long

2427.
two days of radioactive high-voltage wire spirals
you x-rayed my secrets
I returned washed clean to the bone

2428.
maybe there's nothing I can do about it
maybe I always saw you coming
maybe I stood here and waited

2429.
you people all play mean
you know exactly what you are doing
your bright-red-lipsticked mouths mock and
        mesmerize me

2430.
a slight guilty conscience
just the usual follow-up nightmares
sleep under the watchful eyes of the vultures

2431.
We hold on to something unusual
something no one values but us
We've already said yes.

2432.
the city sidewalk staccato stiletto dance troupe
I love the tapping of our skinny heels on concrete
the thrill of running all-out for a bus

2433.
Splot the tomato in my hair and call me a
        tossed salad?
Just try it and see where it gets you
I'll sauté all of you and grill your ears.

2434.
The electricity in this house is so cluttered
I'm twitching at jolts I can't anticipate
The charged air whirls around me.

2435.
Then one day I was free as a bird
no regrets but not no regrets either.
Just free.

2436.
The empty silver casserole dish
me looking into it
my bloated reflection staring back

2437.
the memory
now broken into fragments
I liked that world the way it was

2438.
trust me I can tell you
he has the right kind of background
if you are looking for monotony and a taste for
          loud music.

2439.
the thunder and a few licks of rain
chased me down the street
a stray cat watching me from a doorstep

2440.
the gold mine
snapping its mouth open and shut
so what's your guess it said
Get rich quick or not?

2441.
she is up to something
crushing the ice with her teeth
the juice staining her lips red

2442.
See the last house on the right
if only I had not opened the door
let that cat out
I'd still have my left leg

2443.
Not one tooth in my head
ever liked this dentist
I had no idea until one day they bit him

2444.
moving day everything packed
two jars of grape jelly
overlooked in a cabinet

2445.
gargle-voiced
not gargoyle
you idiot

2446.
the whole building shook
I had no idea
you could laugh so hard or so long

2447.
two new files
I don't know what's in them
I began to think of the damage

2448.
a little nervous
buttoning my sweater
I can't match up the two sides

2449.
she's gone upstairs
trailing a river of lava
melting the ice in your veins

2450.
a pile of dust in the upstairs hall
I had no idea how attached to it I had become
until one day it was gone

2451.
in the void
a few small screws holding things together
mean everything

2452.
Sewing machine
the needle punches
the fabric writhes
the thread tangles

2453.
we made this deal a long time ago
don't you ever wonder
what you'll do without a soul?

2454.
a bruised knee
some aggressive choice of phrasing
Dad climbing out of the basement window

2455.
the freezing carbon dioxide atmosphere
the color running from the sky in the rain
I had no idea how beautiful the afterlife could be

2456.
the neon sign flickers
as if the building were breathing
I open the door and walk in

2457.
slithering
in a sway kind of mood
it's what you see reflected in my eyes

2458.
the bedroom was dark and damp
no reprieve from the smell
so what's your guess? Mildewed socks?

2459.
I laughed and he followed
he fluttered and I sparked
we were young and good-looking
in no hurry at all

2460.
I'm suggesting
an accusation
not a good-bye tribute

2461.
he's not a cheater
I can tell
yes no maybe

2462.
first they swoop in the vultures and then
what's your name? what's your flavor? they ask
when you cry salty tears they shake red pepper on you

2463.
I never saw it coming
her glorious lilac-green smile
a private paint brand straight from her heart

2464.
I am not just a machine
all sparking wires and fizzing fuses
I am vengeful. It will be so rewarding
to say good-bye to you.

2465.
a crustacean at the buffet
everyone saw it but I'm the one who stuck out my plate:
Sweetheart, will you dance with me?

2466.
that's all the info I need:
smart
complicated
single

2467.
two side pockets
no proof of any money
in either of them

2468.
yes she did
I'm not sure why
because of course
I did not.

2469.
he said she said is all we've got
it's easy to be a story that doesn't end
but where does it get you?

2470.
the boss
his obviously fake fainting spell
when I asked for a raise

2471.
hop and be quick about it
an insalubrious turn of events at our place of business
now we're playing musical chairs to see who gets
          laid off

2472.
So who is this and do you remember
it's a perfect set-up
for hurting someone's feelings
because you don't. Remember, I mean.

2473.
you told me
Let me pave the way for you
You leaped to drive the steamroller
A letter of recommendation would have been
          plenty sufficient.

2474.
I've had my share of fistfights
My version of a slinky social patter
adjusted for the location and the company

2475.
I'll feel worse before I feel better
I'll be so sorry yet one more time
I see exactly how it all works, my old friend

2476.
at the intersection
I no longer remember who you're supposed to be
four down or thirty-three across?

2477.
you have the problem I have the answer
erase the tape
no one finds out

2478.
two bracelets
roll under the refrigerator
no one ever finds out

2479.
my dear not entirely stupid family
you have so much to gain
keep yourself on my good side

2480.
I label all the files
I don't keep secrets
from me

2481.
I don't ask you to keep secrets for me
go home
my soul is no business of yours

2482.
you are so much in fashion
tuna sandwich
I said yes before you even asked

2483.
people who are sick
yelling at the doctor:
make it go away

2484.
one really good life is all I want
the time ticks by
it looks less and less likely

2485.
I don't like strangers
each one is too much of a fresh start
I no longer have the heart for

2486.
we work hand-in-glove
our fingers
scratching on the screen door in unison

2487.
That's the last thing I want
a peculiar sense of something going wrong
a marble falling gently down the inside of my spine

2488.
Everyone knew that it was not real, that
the outlines were a little uncertain
But because they loved him
they complimented his looks

2489.
because it was easier
thinking of nothing
that's what I'll choose again today
said the zero in the tens column

2490.
Did I have any of those cookies last night?
No, because I'm divorced.
You know what I mean.

2491.
the lighted window
the man in the gray suit stood illuminated
esteemed college professor picking his teeth

2492.
the meaningless little story she told
like an envelope full of blank papers
lots of volume nothing conveyed

2493.
I was up all night thinking about it
your deep-dish fried meatballs platter
and not in a good way either

2494.
She's asking me one more time to forgive you.
It's all very touching.
I'm asking you one more time to drop dead.

2495.
An excellent strategy, trout friends
sit tight and zip your lip
Because it's all just fishing, I tell you.

2496.
in those days on occasion
she pretended to be my girlfriend
with no sign of an uneasy conscience

2497.
polished cotton
pacing out the distance
how many years can a seat cover last
on a rarely-used dining room chair

2498.
noodles in green sauce
a well-rehearsed conspiracy
hiding out in a soup tureen safe house

2499.
stealing only cash
since it was so much fun
sleeping on a pillow stuffed with Benjamins

2500.
thank me all you want
the mouse you stepped on
sure won't.

2501.
The off-the-shoulder dress displaced
Conjecture turned to fact
in the most embarrassing way

2502.
Fraud after fraud
No end to our unsavory activities
Fabrications and mix-ups every which way
Our life is perfect. Who knew things could be
        this good?

2503.
Last weekend's party clothes
sleeping it off
in the laundry room

2504.
the silver teapot
your old friend
as pompous as ever

2505.
I have no leverage
little buttercup
my plan didn't work
forgive me.

2506.
Another one fired yesterday
The rest of us fight on
Who will be the last ex-employee?

2507.
everything is tainted now
if I ever hear your voice again
I will have to pretend I didn't.

2508.
a green apple
the catalyst
if you want to leave then let's say good-bye.

2509.
a coffee and two bagels on the table
a skinny latte and two croissants on the table
a vase of daffodils introduces them

2510.
pink fluffy yarn
having second thoughts
knotting rather than knitting

2511.
I was a non-threat a half-hour ago
said the termite
but now I've moved to your house

2512.
there is a secret and I preserve it
I manage the light switch
that keeps you in the dark

2513.
I put my cards on the table
I look you straight in the eye
Nothing lasts.

2514.
on my doorstep and with a tray
a plate of stew with a peculiar odor
I'm having second thoughts about our new neighbor

2515.
staring at the frog
it's just not enough
you really do have to kiss it

2516.
I'm a very pretty face
sniveling
behind a desk

2517.
a toothache in the middle of the night
a kind woman in white coat and pajamas
my dentist to my rescue

2518.
None plus one plus nothing
None of the choices is good
One of the choices plus nothing of the choices is better

2519.
I can sing
my publicist's opinion
notwithstanding

2520.
one big saucy
bowling ball
I flex five fingers I roll strike after strike

2521.
three of my friends
three million shares of stock
I forgave them after three years

2522.
the mystery herself
off in the distance
sitting on the grass

2523.
the man in black knee socks
just part of the crowd of men
in black knee socks

2524.
it's not just bloat
he's healing from a facelift
let him down gently he thinks no one knows

2525.
the empty house
on the highway out of town
bonsai in a blue pot
dead in the front window

2526.
we admitted what we did
we had a big laugh about it
it was just that one lie wasn't it?

2527.
the biography of
the man speaking in a low voice
always elusive

2528.
don't miss the opportunity
come see me in the cemetery
I'll be sitting on your headstone

2529.
unscrew the pipe
put your ear to it
now tell me if you don't feel stupid

2530.
Sour and sophisticated
the both of us were.
I said I wasn't sorry about a day of it but I am.

2531.
A vendetta in the office.
Just what I was in the mood for.
I so delight in holding grudges.

2532.
I think about nothing
the nicer version of it
the one written out in large looping syllables

2533.
a half-hour ago
in the birdbath
the chickadee swam his one-millionth lap.

2534.
she pulled the same scam on me
sold me a whole street of those cardboard houses
the cat stepped on the board
my whole investment was wiped out

2535.
it was just the one word
but
enough to make the alphabet cringe in shame

2536.
seven days in a saltshaker
I never thought I'd get through it
it was one heck of a shaker-down

2537.
I agree with you
alarm clock
it's very early

2538.
Now you're so happy
as long as no one changes the rules
you'll stay that way

2539.
Bad weather
why can't you divide it
save some of it for later throw it out mail it away?

2540.
what it feels like to the client:
one more unpleasant
oof right in the stomach

2541.
leaves on the ground
in the air
it will end with me in the cemetery

2542.
the man I am today
the one I made clean
did he lie to me?

2543.
highflying golden kites
pink clouds at sunset
like greasy potato chips in a punch bowl

2544.
he was sobbing at the sight
enough to water ten thousand pansies
and the truth is I still didn't care

2545.
looping handwriting
stay clear of it
those bulbous l's and o's careening along out of control

2546.
that other problem
save it for tomorrow
right now what we need is a hole-free parachute

2547.
as you may recall the insurance company said
did you find that something to laugh about
because we didn't

2548.
the knife in the drawer
the knife in the hand
the filleted business partner lying on the carpet

2549.
To the big eye watching over us
I advise you just to say *Thank You*
Any more than that and you give it ideas

2550.
For the first time
I figure I might be ready to tell the truth
so that I could finally come home

2551.
I'm forever grateful you introduced yourself
because that whole group of lazy-swimming amoebas
never would have bothered

2552.
because two hundred people said so:
the gossip circulated
like holes through Swiss cheese

2553.
backdate the document?
there are second chances, yes
but they usually don't work backwards

2554.
the thumbtacks in a jar
a wedding gift
representing married life

2555.
the postage stamp
set askew on the envelope
the wedding invitation misfolded inside

2556.
In the snow at night
long ago.
It should have been easy.

2557.
baked then deep-fried
then boiled in a vat
that's all I know of that nursery rhyme

2558.
Pssst!
over one block up two floors
come in through the side door
slam it shut

2559.
there is the certainty of it
of something feeling true
as plain as the hands on a clock

2560.
the green leaves
wrapped tight around themselves
one more day of secrets to keep

2561.
the eraser, it was my idea
the descriptive adjective
needed help subduing the noun

2562.
now that we agree about bodybuilders
let's try backhoe drivers
then kosher butchers

2563.
he never missed a day of work
he was a streamlined version of
I need to do it on my own

2564.
and again and again
no more the other than the one
they were such good friends all their lives

2565.
it's a one-time offer
we do that and then we are done
you can only break an egg one time

2566.
if anyone mentions a word of it
remind them that I've got teeth
even if I have no leg to stand on

2567.
is this a joke
this is a joke, right
what if I can't find out if this is a joke

2568.
I think you could make it work
Society needs you to make it work
Press the *Start* button on the washing machine today

2569.
If there's one thing I've learned
Sunglasses
intimidate

2570.
I'm smart
I'm not afraid of you
I'll be of no help to you.

2571.
scorched tingled
coerced snubbed
the engagement is off

2572.
a nasty allegation
three feet of sludge falling on your head
I do so love to spread bad news about you

2573.
sheer fabric
entering the final round of its career
fraying but trying to hold it together

2574.
this stultifying dull party
it's not your fault
but I'm putting a personal eighty-six on it. Let's go.

2575.
Blackmail
somewhere in those boxes
Give it a chance to emerge.

2576.
So I name my price
I arrange it I offer no details
One week later your pre-expired becomes expired.
Deal?

2577.
a skimpy kind of story
a little bit too short
I guess I need to lower the hem on it

2578.
what kind of man are you
I'm sure somebody might be interested
Your type doesn't fetch much of a premium though

2579.
we both know
the person you care about
is whoever comes next on the list

2580.
please pass on the message:
The metaphors are broken but
Straight talk is still up and running

2581.
Like my girlfriend said
I am a three-way tie
for most thoughtless boyfriend of the year

2582.
so about what happened seven years ago
I did what everyone else does
I made it all go away

2583.
the large mirror reveals
an unrelated matter
that should be under investigation

2584.
why are you standing on my porch
a man in a dark suit and blue tie
never more anonymous than tonight?

2585.
I worry
because I made a layer cake
in my sleep

2586.
the rainbow exploded
the pieces
blew through the open window

2587.
it was just a little crime
it should have been easy
all I had to do was focus on the clown

2588.
I hoped for a second chance
the look on your face
told me not to

2589.
a labyrinth
crossing lines
tsk tsk against the rules

2590.
with one word
I incinerate
the fairy tale

2591.
files in reverse alphabetical order
how devious how diabolical
everyday bureaucracy can be

2592.
you taunt me
sleep
you conspire against me

2593.
in a small way
it was so clearly
a great deal of money

2594.
the next person on the list
just baggage in the trunk of the car
as of this afternoon

2595.
sound waves
plus a pencil
shorthand notes fill a page

2596.
cast a spell
these clouds do
their insight is remarkable

2597.
So where have I been?
I guess we'll just have to keep looking
until we found me

2598.
a family reunion
alliances
buried like carrots in the ground

2599.
the professor droned on
a matinee performance on a hot afternoon
the audience slept with their eyes open

2600.
so what's on your menu today
a dash of extortion?
a soupçon of gregarious duplicity?

2601.
think back a few years
if I hadn't let my emotions get the better of me
some of the early photos would show me smiling

2602.
A personal reference.
A threat from the past.
I need you to call me a different name now.

2603.
then two then three
in a fake French accent
So charming. So delicious!

2604.
the same thing I told you yesterday
I want you to come home
I want it not to be a mistake

2605.
see the sun
packing up now
putting the sky in perfect order

2606.
a whole family of shoplifters
their strange gods
so sensitive to price tags

2607.
it's just a moth
very eager to please
born right here in this town

2608.
musical accompaniment
to a slap in the face
could it be some kind of love signal?

2609.
Restless and vengeful
You've mailed a rack-full of greeting cards
each a symbolic slap in the face

2610.
what could you possibly want
in that warehouse on the outskirts of the city
and why do you need to leave work early today?

2611.
in case you didn't notice
five minutes in the past twelve years
is really not a lot of time spent crying over you

2612.
the circuits have an old-fashioned outlook
the wires are just plain tired
it's a problem only because the electrons are young
    and antsy

2613.
They all said the same thing
She can't be all bad?
I never thought of that.

2614.
in the ventilation shaft
butterflies swirl and rise
lost and found me

2615.
so you've been informing on me
but what if I told you the babysitter
is a semi-pro spy herself?

2616.
if I may
I knew it was a mistake
even before you started swimming.

2617.
sizzling green smoke
mmm those cricket squish-kebabs
they sure smell good

2618.
singing a ballad
paddling a canoe
the mood sweeps me along
under a summer moon

2619.
that's my signature tune
performed in my beautiful singing voice
entranced
the lights of the city blink in time with the melody

2620.
usually very considerate and reasonable
our two-car garage
but if I were you I wouldn't be late one minute

2621.
it's a cynical interpretation but
this guy's the only reason
she really means it

2622.
washing his hands
scouring his hands
and probably for nothing
Blood sticks.

2623.
writing the letter this afternoon
I try to hide behind cliché
I burst it at the seams

2624.
the open window
a full plate on the kitchen table
a crow stands on the windowsill

2625.
the hallway
empty
every door closed and locked

2626.
in my apartment on the third floor
a number of past occupants
talk to me in low voices

2627.
did you shrink wrap
the silverware drawer
for any reason in particular?

2628.
those feet
are way too tight
for these ankles

2629.
my two broken ribs
bossy and rude
they keep me up at night

2630.
if for no other reason besides the taxes
and just because he has no other friends
oops I think that's two reasons already

2631.
lay off the cake
froth a couple of radishes into a smoothie
snack on that instead

2632.
I practiced the tap dance routine
in the storage locker
an inspiration that saved my marriage

2633.
there is a lot of traffic today
all its life-threatening shenanigans
messing with my head

2634.
jealous
I'll just double check
yes, I'm still giving you a reason to be

2635.
I'm writing a letter
sitting at my desk crying
I hate working with onionskin paper

2636.
the new guy
has the fat content of a super-sized candy bar
not the good taste, though

2637.
it's all just gossip of course but
in this one-horse town
a new horse naturally blows the roof off

2638.
the ants crawled clockwise on the picnic blanket
the mustard on the hot dogs
first to notice

2639.
a zesty cole slaw recipe
how convenient and how effective a weapon
against the nightmare of cabbage overpopulation

2640.
scold
and scrape fingernails
and cupcake crumbs
under the carpet

2641.
I guess I shouldn't have been surprised
it was so shady under his nose
but I had hoped to get a nice tan on this vacation

2642.
yeah I had a few health problems
after I survived the fracas in the waiting room
but at least I'm still alive and wiggling

2643.
bottle of vanilla in the kitchen cabinet
blue and white tiles in the bathroom floor
a snake crawling out of the sump pump reservoir
all the things that make a house a home

2644.
all that girl does these days is worry
if she didn't know you
you and your choices wouldn't matter

2645.
I know what you think I know.
I've always known it. How I know it?
Let's just say I'm not the nice guy here.

2646.
insubordination is
sleeping on the couch in the living room
right this very minute

2647.
there went your nose again
sorry but the universe had her way
though it really was a last-minute decision

2648.
the celebrity and his publicist passed out in unison
it's all for show
there's no such thing as a too-personal question

2649.
The ultimate in lilac
I am
No offense but you are only pale purple.

2650.
hey you sir I said hey you
stop prancing around like that
let me get a fair shot at your little exoskeleton, you

2651.
I am super beautiful
cultured like a string of pearls
wealthy and an orphan
Please cast me in something besides a romance novel.

2652.
the crack in the sidewalk
the in-between place
where I feel the most comfortable

2653.
the ramshackle speedboat leaped forward
one minute forty-five seconds later
waterskiing downriver in my cutoff shorts and T-shirt
I was outpacing airplanes in the sky

2654.
in her purse
the orange egg
hatched into a civilization-threatening bird of kindness

2655.
first she's been married twenty-eight years and then
she was never married for even one minute and now
she denies she knows what marriage is

2656.
I know you don't like me
Could you maybe be mad at that other guy
Consider taking it out on him?

2657.
step behind me
lopsided moon
let my rain wash clean the roofs of the sleeping town

2658.
threw out the habit-forming painkillers
I knew I couldn't afford to listen
even though their version of the story
sure beat the one my broken foot was telling me

2659.
the orphan
self-made
and no one ever suspected

2660.
common sense I know I'm telling you too late
if only you had bulked up in the gym
these fools wouldn't be able to whip your butt
        all day long

2661.
in your third-floor apartment
your first marriage
detoured itself to the sixth floor a few times too many

2662.
the left eye is the problem
she's not as reliable as she used to be
but thank goodness she still sees your smile just fine

2663.
finally some real
not in front of the kids
language

2664.
remove the pink sofa from my living room
I don't keep secrets
or pink sofas

2665.
bleak look?
sheep look?
I didn't quite catch what you said.

2666.
I am remembered
in snapshots glued to album pages
Why isn't that enough?

2667.
sure it's someone else's fault
but you owe me for the two weeks
I spent digging through your hair follicles

2668.
received a gift certificate for the treatment of an
        impacted molar
I didn't mean to be ungrateful but
I wear dentures

2669.
these high-school girls
believe me you don't know what it's like
driving a bus full of them with no aspirin at hand

2670.
my exit plan
located in my suitcase
A lime-green silk blur I'll be
come midnight tonight

2671.
I thought maybe you could
please do this one thing
start making wedding plans

2672.
be patient
I manufacture suspense
right here in my bedroom

2673.
do the tap dance routine
in work boots if you have to
That's how I've stayed happily married all these years

2674.
not even ten words into the meal
in a dank wine cellar restaurant
and I knew I'd never go out with him again

2675.
so here comes the cat into the library
his cute little mouth clamped down on a dead mouse
ten people tonight will have bad dreams about cats
or about minced mouse

2676.
inchworm
sew tiny stitches
give me time to save up for those new clothes

2677.
in my lime green mood
nothing can discompose me
I love it when the rainbow has time to remember me

2678.
that's the problem with
a lot of eye shadow
think pollen think hay fever it all goes pffft

2679.
no offense but
an outdated hairdo
is as friendly to lice as any other

2680.
I tell myself I will remember
the acronyms
instead I recite the whole alphabet

2681.
a crow
happening along here
told me off

2682.
from now on
vermin
heads up.
I was naïve, not merciful. No more.

2683.
somehow I realized I was onstage
my hands clammy
my digestion gluey

2684.
the doctor couldn't seem to decide
I'm overwhelmed by the details
she said

2685.
your egg-yolk yellow legs
clipped their way through the fog
like flashy scissors cutting wrinkled paper

2686.
skip the hair cut
paint stripper
that would be my idea

2687.
feeling shame
resuscitating a social conscience
empty-headed sycophants on a consciousness-raising
      retreat

2688.
when did the rainbow turn its attention to you
jealousy
assigning you the space between yellow and blue?

2689.
the refrigerator's small clicks and rattles
something less than inconsequential
something more than maddening

2690.
I saw differently through the cracked window
the view broke open your soul for me
a dark streak split you right above your eyelids

2691.
I am asleep
I am safe in the murk of unconsciousness
I am a snail curled inside my shell

2692.
it's just one lunch
it's just one new recipe
I'm sorry it gave your stomach acid such a workout

2693.
high-fashion head to toe
but I was looking for
a more primal connection

2694.
It was half a lifetime ago
I first set my eyes on you -
How things have changed since then.

2695.
when I tell you I can do you seventy percent of a favor
what I am saying is
our relationship is a tire losing air going flat

2696.
the smell of a bad suggestion
the whiff of your curdled reputation
you wicked rotten egg
stay away from my cake

2697.
a chronic illness
bluffing medications
bent on a good solid revenge

2698.
if I had realized
no one is that stupid
I would have known I was that stupid

2699.
in mint condition
a side effect of
no reader having ever opened your latest book

2700.
screams from the haunted house
a tin can rattling down the deserted street
the scrawny cat sighed in boredom

2701.
I certainly don't regret
I ever met you
two million untraceable dollars ago

2702.
oh, it's just a salty way of saying
now we'll do things my way
the tour guide told the terrified tourists

2703.
I was jealous and idle
my life was an expensive hobby
it has always been a risk to know me

2704.
those vexatious handwritten letters
how good are you
at sweeping up broken syllables?

2705.
I judge it an apt phrase for her:
selfish reckless and disaster-prone.
Usually the auguries are not so forthright.

2706.
singing a duet
on a double-date
with the wrong partner
oh boy

2707.
the silver railing
on the top floor balcony
a forgotten can of root beer balances there

2708.
it's good to make a friend
peculiar two
better than oddball one?

2709.
a coat style very popular this season
steamed green the color
the cut a modified snow pea silhouette

2710.
wash your dirty laundry
while the clothes are still on you -
you do know I use bleach on everything?

2711.
the musical score
is running a little late
the orchestra has beaten it to the finish

2712.
I thought I could handle it
that two-minute conversation
disguised as a power-washing

2713.
Dinosaur eggs
perforated
Prehistoric pysanky themes would be appreciated

2714.
I hold a single red rose
in my high school prom picture
my right thumb thorn-impaled and bleeding

2715.
I could spend hours enjoying the panoramic view
over the extensive landscape
of my charmed life

2716.
my summer job standing on the sidewalk
serenading passers-by
on the merits of expansive hair products

2717.
the saint's mitten
dropped in the snow
a handful of zinnias surrounding it

2718.
I dream of dinner reservations
just the two of us
instead here we are once again
hatchet-throwing with your work buddies

2719.
a cup of black coffee
a slice of chocolate layer cake
It's a good impulse. Obey it.

2720.
of course we'll get married I heard him say
Even better
I could actually see his lips move

2721.
like cheap gloves all stretched out
exactly the kind of personality we need
to round out our management team

2722.
sweeping up the broken glass
of small talk
at the end of that splintered day

2723.
the second kitten
younger and angrier
a whole lot more in a smaller package

2724.
on the bottom of the pool
silver beads in two strands
encircle a small dead frog

2725.
the unending incautious hilarity
so much a part of filing papers
all day in a windowless storage room

2726.
the handwritten message
illegible words in blue ink
bloom on a rain-soaked paper
discarded in the street

2727.
the five clouds
crawling away from the horizon
in furtive silence.

2728.
winter grasped me
with both hands
malicious cold and heartless

2729.
this chameleon of a woman
angry because she liked being angry
until she didn't like being angry

2730.
this very green and quiet night
peeled open and the rind tossed aside
the succulence of it heavy on the lips

2731.
I ask you to lie for me.
The face behind the grimy window
it could have been anyone, right?

2732.
a man like me in the prime of life
way too soon
becomes the old geezer wearing high-waisted pants

2733.
I'm getting way too old for
a roomful of men
all wearing black-rimmed glasses

2734.
I give you my solemn word
I can't promise you
I can do the least legal thing to help you

2735.
events not operating in favor of
the very small teacup
now lying in pieces on the tile floor

2736.
this wedding-dress headache
if only it would shrink two sizes
the headache not the dress

2737.
it took me more than ten years
to get to this blessed day in which I finally have
nothing on the agenda

2738.
my mood is
a pearl -
a pink one.

2739.
next in line and ready to make salad history
the most competent avocado
you have ever met

2740.
oh, my dear
there is no need for muscles
once your joints have rusted

2741.
I'm not ashamed of myself
Tomorrow will not make me so
if today has not

2742.
thunderstruck and
wearing a pink and white apron -
that is how I will always remember you

2743.
plural guesses
sleeping under a question mark
keeping each other company

2744.
the frozen lake:
ice cube tray
of some considerable heft

2745.
My brother in a predicament
Multiplied so many times
I've had to make a spreadsheet to keep up

2746.
I'm a pane of clear glass
you say the rock-throwing was an accident
I say it was attempted murder

2747.
in case anyone cares about promises made fifty
        years ago
let me hide the letters
under this loose floorboard

2748.
funny
everything seems to be happening
in that other file cabinet

2749.
I'll make a few phone calls
manipulate some friends
the Hammer walks again

2750.
there is not even one question
I can answer
about solving cryptic crossword puzzles

2751.
I've recently decided to let go of the ugly past
What's the disinfection procedure
and may we discuss your fee?

2752.
seen to peel it from the outside in
out of the gloom it emerges
the perfect heart of the sweet onion

2753.
they know all about flattery
this whole roomful of leather chairs
and how they gossip behind your back!

2754.
green-blue eyes in the right light -
oh, when will I be able
to stop looking at her picture?

2755.
No family in this city
My friends lost to the past or buried.
I begin again to fabricate a life.

2756.
You admire my dead-flower corsage:
My heart is nothing but a cold black shell.
It froze the blooms right through my skin.
Beware of falling in love with me.

2757.
no no the cabbage
at the worst possible moment
cast its pale green spell

2758.
ring the doorbell
if a man smoking a pipe answers it
holding a mop in his left hand
give the countersign

2759.
I just need to stand in the sun and the rain.
I just need to put down roots.
I just need you to let me do things my own way.

2760.
I have my bad conscience but
there's no looking back
it's time to dispose of the dead flowers

2761.
I've gotten a better offer
I'll take half if there is one less
all rolled into one. Got it?

2762.
an episode
involving a small pink pincushion:
my thinking is we all have things we are ashamed of

2763.
so when you tell me
he looked me in the eye
I want to know: Which one of my eyes
do you think it was?

2764.
it's hard to put big problems into reverse
a dozen kitchen sinks
not enough to clean up this mess

2765.
I'm taking notes
in the hopes that someday I will realize
you have owed me a favor for years

2766.
he gave me his business card
big ego
bluffing in the fine print

2767.
the black cat and maybe
I don't know what your angle is
but I think it was a fake black cat

2768.
I've been holding on to this grudge
I no longer have the receipt from where I got it
I guess after this long I can't return it anyway

2769.
a short walk
a paper clip in my pocket
all right. let's get busy making some money.

2770.
my toes
two dozen of them
and I'm still not through counting

2771.
a middle-aged dining room table
certainly over the age of forty-five
a realist about what life really holds

2772.
a cash offer is more dangerous.
I like getting in and out of trouble.
I'll take you up on it. Hit me.

2773.
two doctors and four times
I sat in the waiting room for six hours
eight seconds is all took for them to bill me

2774.
a tirade against
weak coffee
congealing in a cracked mug

2775.
disorientation occurring
at the worst possible moment
for such a kinetic person

2776.
a fresh new mop
self-assured
with no fear of career success

2777.
dear diary
I write on the pages front and back
in all our years together you have never betrayed me

2778.
I put myself through another cake-baking session
believe me
what a purple ego-popper I produced

2779.
you asked me to marry you
maybe I do agree
maybe we could get a second opinion

2780.
You have forced me to see myself as I really am
I curse you
and your shiny shaved head

2781.
refill the coffee pot
some serious karaoke this weekend coming up
I sing better when I'm working off solid caffeine jitters

2782.
I've got two chocolate doughnuts in this bag -
a second attempt
to start over again

2783.
I needed money
so I cast a spell on the bank
Every deposit ticket on Tuesday had my name on it.

2784.
I'm going on a little trip
to pick up a dropped penny
that's all they told me. Check out my forged passport.

2785.
on the car radio
a program that asks
how can you nullify this snafu that you find yourself in?

2786.
it's very simple as I recall it:
over and over you say mean things and then apologize
then you get angry that I give up on you

2787.
before you decide it's just not worth it
look into my head
glimpse the difference it will make to me

2788.
Buried in errors
I gave up too quickly.
That's who I am these days.

2789.
I need the theatrics of a handshake deal
I need to polish the leaves on the trees in the park
I need something to laugh about in nine different cities
Let's not save it for tomorrow. Let's start tonight.

2790.
a vintage watch
pancaked
on the concrete

2791.
it's crucial to
the lady in the pink linen suit
that you find nothing to laugh about in her presence.

2792.
I am too marvelous.
I am irresistible. I am style. All are drawn to me.
I am like greasy potato chips to a line of ants.

2793.
the descriptive adjective
boiled in a vat
limp and mushy

2794.
the big green wrench
the perfect match for my husband's big green head
Could it really be just this easy?

2795.
I'm remembering a summer long ago
a single room facing the alley
a hotel lobby full of wedding guests

2796.
in this line of work
we must handle things gently
Therapist? No, furniture delivery man.

2797.
the key to the back door
has a very strong connection
to our success in gaining entry to the kitchen

2798.
laundry problems, said the surgeon, certainly not
the spine is intricate, true
but knitted in washable wool

2799.
angle it up a little, she said
as she painted
your kneecap

2800.
rattle the spoon
against the lip of the idol
it may seem insensitive but it's what he likes

2801.
striding along the iron lines
striking a pose at the railway station
the handsomest hunk of diesel I ever saw

2802.
stay in bed tall blond woman.
you can forget about your job.
you will win the lottery today.

2803.
seven flights of stairs up through the stairwell
how efficient it is and some extra
if you want to go to the seventh floor

2804.
legally changed my name
never realized I would miss
the incessant wisecracking

2805.
A few of life's big questions
I shrank them down in the hot water wash
Now help me fold them please

2806.
Check the cash in your purse
I am turquoise today
So make sure you've got the bail money ready

2807.
the Threes and the Eights say they are 16/17 sure
they are not related no matter how far back you go
but what if you consider the question
on a scale of One to Ten?

2808.
the innuendos were so ungracious
it was so awfully easy for you to pull the strings
of this set of mismatched dancing marionettes

2809.
The boss lying motionless across his desk
I've seen this grandstand play before
of course he's asleep
but the darts in his back are new. Nice touch.

2810.
I'm looking out for my future
you bet those publicity photos
zing

2811.
don't disconnect the pipes yet
just one more bubble bath in the old tub
please

2812.
her thought patterns
misappropriating the disorientations
of the merry-go-round

2813.
let's not judge the chicken
coming in second place
in a two-turtle race

2814.
the in-process pineapple upside-down cake
took advantage of my aunt's gullible nature
rolled over in the oven

2815.
that perpetually aggrieved songstress
her theme song:
Why Do There Have to Be Clouds in My Mirror?

2816.
I'm putting you in charge here
what a great thing for you
As they say
You sure landed in kale didn't you?

2817.
lightning strikes twice
very obliging of it I think
neither of the twins gets left out that way

2818.
she broke the mirror with her hairbrush
retaliation
the mirror for showing her a bad hair day
the hairbrush for doing nothing to fix it

2819.
the red crinkle fabric on a hot streak right now
the leopard-print coming on strong
a deadlock in the cruise ship's dining room formal night

2820.
the needle pulled the pink thread
a cruel journey it had
with no one to break a path for it

2821.
the gears turned and sped up
but knots were untied in the middle
and the love affair fell out backwards

2822.
neighbors here on this side of the street
I tell you they were born saying the phrase
be on the lookout for

2823.
oh you mustard-head
how obvious the answer was
but I guess condiments freeze inside a snow job

2824.
it's only because she intervened
that you are not my homicidal lawfully-wedded
riot and mayhem hunk of a husband
and I'll never forgive her for it

2825.
saucy-living chainsaw of a woman
unquashed by narrow-minded conventional living
I admire her greatly

2826.
I bet you weed-killer
against your poison pen letter
for first-class long-lasting results

2827.
those business associates all six of them
gone by the time you figure it out -
they are not the three wise men times two

2828.
I admit it was my own treasure map
the one I drew so carefully
that betrayed me

2829.
the coral atoll and turquoise lagoon
as metaphor for
a dye-your-hair-change-your-name escape

2830.
Just arrived and you look a little lost
here in this big old dollhouse
My guess is you're the new trophy wife doll?

2831.
in a doom kind of mood
the doctor said *Just a heads up*
You can plan to pick up your uncle's things first
        thing tomorrow

2832.
because people talk and I have secrets
I don't stress any syllable and I spell out nothing
I'm not specific and I don't fill in the colors

2833.
Campfire rule: let me remind you
squelch the flashlight
if you want to get straight to the spooky
in the ghost-outside-the-tent stories

2834.
I refuse to
participate in a plotline in which
I cry myself to sleep each night

2835.
the gods have put their mark on me
the contract is in the desk drawer
I am no longer saving for my retirement.

2836.
I see now I shouldn't have assumed the
skewered-with-a-set-of-engraved-steak-knives option
was off the table

2837.
is there any chance
we can become strangers again
go back to when we each were lonely but at peace?

2838.
I've been waiting for a sign
plus or minus, either one is fine
but I need to know if he is sleeping or is he dead

2839.
the audacious
pink peonies
at twilight

2840.
this blouse
it fights dirty
it has the audacity

2841.
write to me won't you
like we did in the old days
the discretion of it is so appealing

2842.
throw your whole heart into that power struggle
or
get up and start running for your life

2843.
to be kind about it she sang well out of tune
but to a roomful of friends
thankfully susceptible to suggestion
who applauded when I did

2844.
I was never nutty enough to think
one cathartic phone call
would finish the job

2845.
Some of the people are guessing
but some of the people know.
Look for me on the bottom of the lake.

2846.
she has as much influence as
a paper clip
in a junkyard

2847.
clear the deck
your moment in the innuendo sun has run out
now give some of the other loudmouths a turn

2848.
a discreet and dignified man
who did odd jobs around town
the anonymous holder of all the secrets

2849.
the recurring nightmare
a hazard zone unmarked
you stumble into it over and over again

2850.
I did it
it was me
it was for me
I think it's all psychological.

2851.
twirl
that shiny euphoric purple umbrella
and laugh at the rain

2852.
fiction and reality
the sabotage of our secret
but who says we can't exchange one mask for another?

2853.
I'd like to meet in person
untangle the past and the present
but it would break your heart.

2854.
I threw cold water on your idea
to my shock it hissed
forgive me for ever doubting you

2855.
the vexing failure of the murder plan
but it's not all for nothing
Every time we get closer to success.
So who's next up that staircase?

2856.
a glass of champagne a miscalculation
she gets caught up in the mood
her head spins a half-turn and clanks to a stop

2857.
a seven-layer omelet of a ring
citrine emerald
sizzling in a pan of pearls

2858.
Your battered well-worn poem
I can stitch up the side seams
but the verses will no longer align

2859.
the recent file room snafu kicked it off
the whole long con set in motion
next up three nuns and a squabble on the bus

2860.
Three minutes stretched out like a rubber band
that one enchanted evening just last night
but today is the snap-back.

2861.
that happy story
left sparkles around the mouth
of each person who passed it on

2862.
in a hospital bed
in a fine pickle
in a too-small gown wide open at the back

2863.
the incoming asteroid
sparkly slinky swishy
wearing zinc earrings and looking for trouble

2864.
My only chance
to be one of the two of us
It's right now. Please say yes.

2865.
who is this person
doing all the things other people do
but so much more convincingly?

2866.
arm muscles
you sure talk a lot
the day after I up the weights at the gym

2867.
like the minister said at the wedding
take two people just semi-broken in
marriage will polish them right up you bet

2868.
see she's got another mind
tucked right behind the front one
then there's her secret backup stashed behind the
          refrigerator

2869.
a million new brain cells
sleeping in small transparent units
worker bee pupae

2870.
are you nervous about
how I see it
or what I do about it?

2871.
The twinkle in his eye
a myriad of sparkly facets
I didn't like it. Not any part of it.

2872.
almost anywhere in this city you can find
a woman in a black dress and pink pearls
living a complicated story

2873.
skip the squabbles
grab the tweezers
I'll settle things now. Give me your nose.

2874.
after the bus accident
the one word is seasick
since I refuse to commute by bus anymore

2875.
a fault line
the geologist in me can't believe it
but the wife in me does

2876.
Call me fate:
sometimes I like to make surprise visits.
you, you're going to get a promotion.
you, you're under arrest.

2877.
a man like him
with a smile showing a lot of teeth
will not tell the truth even under oath.

2878.
my skimpy damp bathing suit
hissing
in the hot sun

2879.
all my fresh smooth hours
knotted up
ever since I first heard your name

2880.
well I wondered
how can I cope with this disagreeable woman
when her every word is a snarl of white soft string?

2881.
a real smart lawyer
a vulture on a perch
piecing together what you said
with what people heard

2882.
in the dryer the collar of the pink shirt
wrapped itself a little tighter
around the pair of gray socks

2883.
the boat
the topaz ring
years of outdoing each other
together now on the bottom of the bay

2884.
He is
a novel
with not even one chapter finished

2885.
I say to you who is this person
with my initials
on his keychain?

2886.
are you an enzyme on the loose
a lucky hunch stranded
a maze with transparent walls?
Who are you?

2887.
I may have underestimated that girl
she took apart the jet engine
with nothing but a wrench and her own
        sophisticated brain

2888.
as far as this dinner goes
there's no making up with me
ask the waiter to bring the check.

2889.
fifteen years of experience
putting dinner on the table
I'd like to forget about every bit of it.

2890.
take some kind of coincidence
attribute it to fate or religion
or just say it's all part of the big pink happy

2891.
all of you stop shouting
those big shards of glass
are just lonely wandering silica ghosts

2892.
this is the most recent picture of him -
him and his six heads needing haircuts.
I should have gotten rid of it
but he's got such nice smiles, I just couldn't.

2893.
a zig-zag of a tale
that diagonal kind of language
where you sort of slide up and sit beside the meaning

2894.
I say your name
must be thirty forty times every day
always with a light satisfied flutter
of my happy heart

2895.
On Tuesdays they offer
a free courtesy asphyxiation
of your worst enemy
only if you get him/her there by noon

2896.
on a spa vacation for two weeks
he went away flat and punched down
an efficient reshaping fluffed him back into form

2897.
knowledge and discernment
on a non-stop flight
up there inside his very roomy brain

2898.
on official business
the two arrows
took care of the loose ends

2899.
inherited wealth
a necktie owner
not a necktie wearer

2900.
the pearl and sapphire necklace
a lasso
around my neck

2901.
the ego of the man
who isn't a lifeguard
shirtless on the job

2902.
where in town might one find
a job for the well-adjusted virus?
I do good work.

2903.
in the alcove
a witness to that terrible deal I made
the piano with its cover closed over the keys

2904.
not paying my bills
is on my to-do list
for next week

2905.
swear to me
you didn't bake this cake
while the fumigators were doing the kitchen

2906.
a gallon or two of yellow smear
mixed in the blender
it's going to surprise a few people

2907.
your colleagues
fifty/fifty
rattlesnake/nothing but fizz

2908.
the midnight voicemail
a little bit creepy
but mostly self-conscious

2909.
broke my heart
a long time ago
with the small things you didn't do

2910.
Eight feet tall
in prime condition.
Yes. Lock the window now.

2911.
The pancakes on the plate
she threw them right over the balcony rail.
There is no decoder ring for this marriage.

2912.
Tired of too-big smiles and swagger
I packed my life in a suitcase
I hope the train is right on time.

2913.
since I first heard your name
since I first saw your pale blue eyes
since I first felt my skin crawl at the sound of your voice

2914.
I reflect your *sorry* back on you
from the angry depths of the mirror I've become:
I stab you blind with the shards of your pale words

2915.
It's a little bit noir in here tonight
a black and white herringbone kind of night.
We need lights and music. Get out the cocktail shaker.

2916.
My name is Mrs. Pumice
the enchantress. I know more about everything
than you do.
Cross me and I will chew you with my big yellow teeth.

2917.
I'll stop by after work
hair done
fangs all polished up

2918.
the sound of
her grandmother's pearl necklace
scattering itself on the tile floor

2919.
she likes her fiancés
served in individual packets
she's fine right now thank you but maybe
one more later

2920.
Argentinian boyfriend
a full moon
too few movies start off this way

2921.
I'm almost positive
I'm only semi-negative
I'm more than annoying

2922.
quite imaginative they are
the factoids
at getting noticed

2923.
intentional forgetfulness
blurring the lines
I hide my real self

2924.
Depressed
cash at a low ebb
losing interest

2925.
I read graffiti on the bathroom wall
I wonder if it means me
I have to know the answer
I write a request for more info.

2926.
Use your Indiglo watch
to find your way out of your boyfriend's basement
when his wife comes home early

2927.
the fire-siren decibel levels
of Banshee Screaming Screecher-Red Lipstick
oh it's just right for the me mood I'm in

2928.
we were college friends
tying up the loose ends
of old times gone and best forgotten

2929.
the multiple contusions
on my bank account
the result of you putting the squeeze on me

2930.
the feeble gleam of the car's headlights
the dog barking
the muted sparkle of the steady rain

2931.
the fog
asphyxiating
my sense of recklessness

2932.
floating in the black ocean
the jewel in the moon's navel
glows a dark aquamarine

2933.
get out the instructions and read the footnotes
maybe you'll find a snafu
you can insert yourself into

2934.
I was real I was alive
four days ago
it's hard to believe all I am today
is a corpse listening to my eulogy

2935.
Any place you want, you say, there we'll go
I twist the knob I choose
last week

2936.
a corner of the world
this moment of envy
that I couldn't afford to examine too closely

2937.
no matter how much imagination you have
she is still just a dead person
singing sad songs on the radio

2938.
the way you surprised me
it gave me the biggest shock
since the werewolf thing I mean

2939.
a few people and drinks after work
emotional lava flowing
who's going to mop up all the sloppy at the
        office tomorrow?

2940.
the pins and needles
nigh crazy with relief
rushed home to their tomato-shaped pincushion

2941.
it was torture experiencing
your logic
crawling a zig-zag worm trail in my head

2942.
for weeks in that room
I practiced the piano
pounding away until the paint peeled from the walls

2943.
He wants to revisit Glasnost
You know
in Scotland

2944.
red shoelaces rein in the foot
the yellow-marigold of the skirt fabric
tangles around the leg

2945.
screaming three times was just the start of it
when I heard they'd be here tomorrow morning
planning on staying for a few weeks

2946.
there is a market for rational answers
but what if
I don't have any questions

2947.
no one looks into
easy dreams
the way they really ought to

2948.
did the cat lick the bowl already
or will I be the early bird that gets the worm
this morning?

2949.
a romantic weekend
with an orphan
by the river in the fog
That's the plot.

2950.
meet me in the laundry room
the pink spin cycle
has to be seen to be believed

2951.
my speech to the shareholders
greed and synergy
greed and synergy
synergy and greed

2952.
in theory
the funeral
puts an official end to being described as alive
        and well

2953.
the previous night
answers to pertinent questions
finally sputtered in

2954.
the saint now gone to the dark side
spat out animosities
in a spray of red spittle

2955.
I left the office
with a referral for a better boyfriend
with a prescription for a different plotline in my
        next romance

2956.
In today's world the crystal ball
finds itself at a loss
more often than it likes to admit

2957.
the blade of the lawnmower
the blade of grass
they meet and that's where things go sketchy

2958.
tresses grow don't they but
Rapunzel
show me any kind of proof it could really
        happen this way

2959.
my sense of recklessness
metallic and brittle
the nail that breaks off when the hammer hits it

2960.
my priority is
that healthy kind of guy
who is upstairs right now

2961.
following the directions I (insert disclaimer and explain):
I don't make decisions
I assemble experts

2962.
creepy and unsettling
that green plaid sofa
moved in a year ago
hasn't stopped eyeing me since

2963.
Today let's
solve the equations for X
and chocolate eggs and rain
and the movements of your toes

2964.
misuse of a ladder
gravity and broken ribs
and on a Tuesday to boot

2965.
twelve fake years and
how we imagined they were -
well sunshine that's how it's going to play

2966.
when you close your eyes
the air vents in your eyeballs
keep your overheated imagination
from exploding your head

2967.
It's because I am so singing that
I would and I did
but not before today
and only this one time

2968.
exhaustion is what I'm calling it
but I must face the truth:
no power lawnmower can cut grass forever

2969.
eye of lemon in the sky
the sea
a sheet of blue paper

2970.
one finger
- come to think of it there is always only one -
presses the *Start* button

2971.
cautious feet
in exquisite shoes
mount the steps to the front porch

2972.
did they argue one more time
did they remember one more time
that they had promised one more time
not to argue one more time

2973.
more than a few people
crossed off the list
because that's what they deserved

2974.
I have limited familiarity
with the truth
Is that it in the living room sleeping on the couch?

2975.
three assistants
a frying pan
a raw sock soaked in egg and breadcrumbs
        ready to go

2976.
a few shouted insults
two people half-asleep
a phone call in the middle of the night
wrong number.

2977.
she resembles
a factory smokestack
complete with cell towers

2978.
a pyramid
that meets all the usual criteria for a superlative
        afterlife
and in today's fresh colors

2979.
please excuse my complete lack of manners
I know I may be getting a bit personal
but I love how your dark blue feet splay out

2980.
this recipe is really special
it includes cage-free chlorophyll
AKA oak leaves

2981.
you really want me to tell you
we haven't done anything silly
when right this minute
we're dyeing your hair in my garden shed?

2982.
is it too soon
for me to disappear
into the fog?

2983.
the last time I held a wrench
it was because it gave me some peace of mind
besides, he really had it coming

2984.
the shock and disbelief
of a blue coffee mug
tumbling toward the tile floor

2985.
a ballerina on stage
no spoilers but
four minutes into the dance...

2986.
My plan
a leaky boat
almost floating

2987.
The scrapbook
was indexed
That photo was never going to stay buried

2988.
we always said
he's everything we hoped to leave behind
until we did and we realized
he's everything we can't afford to leave behind

2989.
how can I accept the color scheme
of this disorderly and disturbing the peace living room
when it won't stop shouting and thrashing around?

2990.
did he weep light tears
or
is that just a rising mist?

2991.
I'm nervous about the next eight hours
the seven days from last Wednesday
the six seconds separating me from a happy ending

2992.
I always advise my clients
leave in a hurry
if the whole amnesia bit doesn't work

2993.
behold and look at me
because a lot of planning has gone into this dress
including potential tax breaks and investment credits

2994.
choose one in three
the acorn the raindrop
the leaf the downpour
the oak the rainbow

2995.
two cans of orange spray paint
on a hot streak
through the highway underpass

2996.
high dive at the outdoor pool
illustrations of the binary explanation of life
either you take the plunge or you don't

2997.
a conversation that could really change a person
at the Lilly Bug Club downtown
if you've got the courage
to have dinner with me there tonight

2998.
red candy-striped petunias and
a pink gingham apron and
cherry popsicles in the freezer
those days are gone forever

2999.
she has a way about her
a nice sense of being feline
a sleek way of padding down the hall
the click of her claws to remind you

3000.
Lighten up sweetheart
sure you feel conflicted but
it doesn't hurt the tweezers at all
not so certain about the splinter, though

3001.
inhale
play along with the game
that's how you make friends in this town

3002.
a piano in the living room
comes with a lot of side effects
tuneless headaches and ringing ears

3003.
it's a big planet
fold it in half
smooth out the wrinkles
loneliness has made

List of Little Vines by Date Written

Date	Number
12/13/2018	2007-2040
12/20/2018	2041-2061
12/27/2018	2062-2086
1/3/2019	2087-2118
1/10/2019	2119-2153
1/17/2019	2154-2187
1/24/2019	2188-2215
1/31/2019	2216-2218
2/1/2019	2219-2250
2/7/2019	2251-2280
2/14/2019	2281-2311
2/21/2019	2312-2337
2/28/2019	2338-2365
3/7/2019	2366-2401
3/14/2019	2402-2432
3/21/2019	2433-2459
3/28/2019	2460-2486
4/4/2019	2487-2513
4/11/2019	2514-2536
4/18/2019	2537-2564
4/25/2019	2565-2593
5/2/2019	2594-2626
5/9/2019	2627-2654
5/16/2019	2655-2682
5/23/2019	2656-2705
5/30/2019	2706-2728
6/4/2019	2729-2730
6/6/2019	2731-2759
6/13/2019	2760-2793
6/20/2019	2794-2812

Date	Number
6/27/2019	2813-2838
7/2/2019	2839-2863
7/11/2019	2864-2892
7/18/2019	2893-2916
7/25/2019	2817-2939
7/31/2019	2940-2969
8/7/2019	2970-3003

66928306R00121

Made in the USA
Middletown, DE
08 September 2019